Lucky Seven

Also by Jordan Smith

*An Apology for Loving the
Old Hymns* (1982)

Wesleyan Poetry

Lucky Seven

Jordan Smith

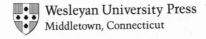

Wesleyan University Press
Middletown, Connecticut

for Malie

Copyright © 1988 by Jordan Smith

Some of the poems in this book appeared originally in *The Antioch Review, Caesura, Grand Street, Ironwood, The Kenyon Review, New England Review/Bread Loaf Quarterly, The Paris Review, Quarterly West, Seneca Review, Shenandoah.* "Days of 1974" first appeared in *Poetry.* The phrase "in isolate flecks" in the poem "Letter to Adrian Frazier" is from "To Elsie" by William Carlos Williams, published in his *Collected Earlier Poems,* ©1938 by New Directions Publishing Corp. and is reprinted by permission of New Directions. The song title "My Back Pages," which appears in the poem "Mandolin," is by Bob Dylan, ©1964 by Warner Bros. Inc., all rights reserved, used by permission. I would like to thank the National Endowment for the Arts and Union College for their generous support, which aided the completion of this book, and Thora Girke for her assistance in the preparation of the manuscript.

All inquiries and permissions requests should be addressed to the Publisher, Wesleyan University Press, 110 Mt. Vernon Street, Middletown, Connecticut 06457.

Distributed by Harper & Row Publishers, Keystone Industrial Park, Scranton, Pennsylvania 18512.

Library of Congress Cataloging-in-Publication Data
Smith, Jordan, 1954–
Lucky seven.
(Wesleyan poetry)
    I. Title. II. Series.
PS3569.M5375515L8   1988   811'.54
ISBN 0-8195-2141-8 (alk. paper)
ISBN 0-8195-1142-0 (pbk. : alk. paper)

Manufactured in the United States of America

First Edition

Wesleyan Poetry

Contents

1

The Confederate Women
  of Maryland 3

Free Verse 7

Fell Street 9

A Sad Pavan for These
  Distracted Times 11

Giorgione: *The Tempest* 12

Alberich 16

Cedar Shoals 18

2

Fragment 25

The Hudson at Mechanicville 26

Auriesville 28

Mandolin 30

A Theater Song for Kurt Weill 34

At Arnold's Monument 37

Days of 1974 40

Burnt Hills 43

Letter to Adrian Frazier 45

3

The Star Chamber   53

Remains   55

Elegy as a Triplet of
  Three-lobed Leaves   57

Country Blues   60

Lucky Seven   63

Notes   71

I

The Confederate Women of Maryland

I haven't seen them for years now,
Those three bronze women who knelt
To comfort a tarnished, fallen
Soldier of the C.S.A.
In a park on North Charles Street,
Just past the Buckingham Arms
Apartments where I lived so
Cheaply that year. Those women,
I was sure, had given up
All but the most formal grief,
And I admired their restrained,
Still ministry, as if they saw
Too far past the crumpled boy,
Past Antietam, Cedar Creek,
Gettysburg, too far to lose
Their dignity in mourning
One poor private. Their heads bowed
Over the Hopkins lacrosse field
Toward Hampden, a neighborhood
Of millworkers, longshoremen,
Temporary help—hicks mostly,
Just off the road from some town
In Virginia or Tennessee.
I'd walk past the row houses,
Old pickups, bars, on my way
To parties in the half-wrecked
Storefront house a friend rented.
The front windows in his place
Were glazed with antique, flawed glass,
And they dimmed the summer glare
To a hazy, slick, almost
Impressionistic shimmer.

I'd stand in the kitchen, smoke,
Sing along with the trumpets
On some forties tune, and watch
The kids from the boarding house
Across the street in their torn
Cycle colors, work boots, tank tops,
Drink stolen quarts on the stoop.
I never thought I'd remember
Hampden, or the tired Chevies
Double-parked in the alleys
Off Ash Street, those kids, steel-mill
Lights above Patterson Park.
My apartment, across town,
Was on a block of churches,
Buildings with out-of-service
Elevators, shabby halls
Behind good facades, police-
Locked doors, a gentle decline
From Roland Park and all those
Tudor and Georgian mansions.
On Sundays, I'd waste hours walking
The aisles of the elegant
Market where even the stock-
Boys and meat cutters wore ties
And were polite to the kind
Old men in worn seersucker,
Who each month lived less and less
Well in the dim, forgetful
Beauty of the avenues.
But what I remember best
Are summer nights, the sirens
On and off again all night

From the rougher streets: Greenmount,
Ash Street. All summer when I
Couldn't sleep in that rich, damp heat
I'd type for hours and hardly
Notice the sirens sounding.
Last week, in a small-town bar,
I watched two brothers, farm boys,
Arm wrestle for shots of rye.
After a few rounds, swearing,
Hoarse, the fat one half stood, slammed
His brother's wrist on the bright,
Splintered edge of an ashtray.
All the locals looked past them,
Out the rain-glazed, smeared windows
Or at the neon waterfall
Shimmering on a beer sign.
But I couldn't stop staring down
At the slight boy, on his knees,
Howling, or at the bottle
He was lifting, somehow,
High, like a broken flagstaff.
And behind him, his girlfriend
Knelt, her face tarnished with shock,
Cradling him, wincing, stupid
With fright and the rigorous,
Still sympathy of a true
Witness. In her silence, in
The sharp house lights flicking on
As the police cleared us out,
She gave up nothing. She had joined
In a confederacy
Of survivors who have seen

Beyond the streaked beauty
Of an American summer
No one they could hope to save.
And those women I admired,
Years ago, on North Charles Street,
Would they have taken nothing
More from that bar, from the dumb
Anger shimmering like noon sun
On the asphalt of Hampden,
Than an aftertaste of rye,
A riff from some big-band tune?
In memory, they seem less grave
Ministers than who they were:
Southern country girls, mothers,
Social ladies, whose hands, raised
As if to ward off the sight
Of that boy's wounds, were caught in
Helplessness, in reverence,
And they did not look away.

Free Verse

In this short-cropped Labor Day
Shock of twilight, the couple upstairs
Are fighting again. From their front porch,
Through the oak trim and plaster

Of this rented duplex flat,
I can't make out just what set them off,
But already, above the private
Syllables, their voices strike

That tense lilt where no excuse
Offered or taken will hold for long.
And already this seems a lesser
Poem than any cry, any

Ragged, habitual fight
Heard late nights through an apartment wall,
Someone's stereo turned high to drown out
The harsh, wrong headlong accents,

Terms of a lease taken
For good or not: to work, pay rent, draft
These lines in the hour after the news,
As if that were the labor of

The pure self, which buys nothing.
As if my words might ease the pained,
Trochaic stumble of my neighbor's
Footfalls on the stairs, the door

Left banging as he walks out
To lose or spend his rage on State Street,
Where the long flights of double houses
　　　Uphill from the turbine plant,

　　　The billboard, blank, above the bank,
The parking lots of the empty stores,
Are transfigured in their slow yielding
　　　To darkness, to circumstance,

　　　To the vacant urban peace
I imagine. Grown tired, graceless
From another interrupted night,
　　　I hope he stays out till dawn,

　　　Hope his wife quits pacing, sleeps.
And later, when they make up, make love,
The bed rattling overhead, quarrels
　　　Half-forgotten as they touch,

　　　Then forgotten—the muffled,
Unmeasured syllables of their fight
Are mine, turned to scansion and account,
　　　Profit of a bad evening.

　　　What's free except forgiveness?

Fell Street

It was no dream. I lay awake
And saw him on Broadway in Baltimore
        Outside the Seamen's Mission.
        His leather jacket torn,
    A welt seaming one lip, he ducked
And wheeled and swore and swore again at no one,

    If it was him, grown so old.
Between us, the crowd of regulars and sailors,
        Rich, slumming kids from Hopkins,
        Pressed like a tide. A whore
    Grabbed at me, swung her hips, sprawled,
Legs wide, against a frightened boy in denim.

    And he was gone, who taught me rye
And chasers, and how the boundaries lay where counter-
        Top diners, churches, bookies
        Shared the row house storefronts,
    Who told me one night what not to say
In that off-hours bar, paid for his shot, looked twice

    Right at the bartender, and said it.
I was alone on a street where the marble stoops
        Were covered with kids' scrawls
        In spray paint, wrappers, slops
    Of beer and chicken from the evening sitters.
Fell Street. One night he said he'd crawl

    Before he set up shop on Fell Street.
Inside the doorway of a Polish bakery,
        Clutching his torn jacket,

9

Young, younger than I,
He stared out at the broken crates
Beside the curb, rust-pitted loading docks,

Then looked at me, looked again, and spat
As I called his name. I woke then—liar
Who knew it was no dream
That I could wake from, liar
Who called him friend in vanity
And carelessness, and left town, left all that.

A Sad Pavan for These Distracted Times

Thomas Tomkins, his elegy for William Lawes, 1649

And now the world you loved turns out of season,
    The best of trees lies wind-blown.
The King is dead. Law and law's reason
        Are overthrown.
        And Lawes, you are dead.
Your brooding fashions, your rare melodies have fled,
    Poor leaves, from Cromwell's treason.

Your loyalty was to the older sadness
    Of mingled song: pavans danced
With courtly airs, grief mixed with gladness,
        With elegance.
        This was art's token,
Which you wore gladly. But now our consorts, broken,
    Play tunes of common madness;

There is no cure. Last night I dreamt a fire
    Swept frozen reeds. Their harsh cries
Untuned my soul, shrieks of loss, higher
        Than ever I
        Could bear. A voice said
We were abandoned, even by our God, for dead.
    Dear friend, that was no liar.

Giorgione: *The Tempest*

Who shall speak first by this stream
Where no one speaks? Waiting, still—the storm's
Confusion of winds not yet striking
    The high-limbed, slender-leaved trees,
    One lightning stroke shearing mid-
Sky toward the provincial capital
Which must seem neither home nor harbor
    To the resting wanderers

Who have not sought shelter there,
But wait, still . . . On one bank, a young man,
Across the stream, a woman, her nursing child.
    Where will they wait out the rain?
    No cover in the slight trees,
The shattered ornamental stones
Of what ruined town, forgotten
    Here beyond the works and days

Of all those whom the painter
Has not rendered, the good townspeople
Who have hurried indoors at the first
    Quickening uncertainty
    Of weather. In their kitchens,
The fires kindled, they drink, and all day
Clouds lower in a dark height of air,
    The long perspective of plains

Foreshortened. Imagine them,
Bitching at the storm, this riverside
Assemblage of dust, smells from the farms,
    A troubled body of air.

As I write, as the weather
Sours, the roof tiles, the marble facade
Of the State Bank and Trust, take on that
    Edgy, uncivil prescience

    Of static between feed ads
And tornado warnings on the all-
Day call-in show from Cedar Rapids.
    Just now I've heard the pure prose
    Of a debt-sick hog farmer,
And a woman who hates her school board,
And a dozen other citizens
    Lost between good faith and rage,

    Nothing in the announcer's
Garbled calm, the AM sputter,
To solve their local apprehensions.
    And the painting on my desk—
    Its argument is wholly
Its own, unanswerable: this town,
With its civic towers and sheltered roof gardens,
    Dreams of peace and upstream trade,

    Might be anywhere at all,
But the man and woman, so intent,
So studied in their indifference
    To the world's unceasing flight
    From their foreground, are always
Elsewhere, standing a little apart,
Figures of a desire as tenuous,
    Unbounded as a landscape

In deep mist. Who shall speak first?
He is dressed richly, carries a staff,
Stands with—is it wonder, arrogance,
    Or assurance; stares toward her,
    In appraisal, passion, joy?
She has left off everything
But the white shawl around her shoulders,
    And is not looking at him,

    Who may be some king's squire
On the prowl, a rich man's prodigal,
A soldier, father to that child.
    These old stories, travelogues—
    Their conjectured, wandered plots
Go on and on, like friends squabbling
Politics in a town bar, solving
    Nothing for hours, never

    Reconciling the hard words
With all the helplessness rooted there.
I don't know who these two are, or why
    I've turned toward them, listening,
    As if they might offer, explain. . . .
This morning, walking the river bank
As the first thunderclaps tried their range,
    Under a clump of willows

    I saw a couple fucking.
I could tell you I just walked away,
But what's ever so simple? I watched
    That light which, before a squall

Breaks across our central plains,
Rises, brilliant and dense, foreshadowing
The storm's quick, full illuminations.
    Sheltering, momentary,

    It glinted on their bodies
As they moved, bore closer, held and fell,
Until they seemed wards of that storm-sky,
    Like the child in the painting,
    Face lost in his mother's breast,
Set apart in undivided will.
I didn't hear their cry. *They* were the words
    For what I wanted, to stand

    A moment where—waiting, still—
Nothing might be explained or resolved.
Then the first rain gust struck the alders,
    And I ran back toward the mall,
    The power plant, the *Daily
Citizen's* wet sandstone block, sidewalks
Slick, empty in a Sunday downpour.
    I might have been anywhere.

Alberich

But in the stippled, rose velvet
Buds of staghorn sumac, in rust-
    Bright veins of briar,
Was a god's hand turned against him,
    Was a god's hatred

Drove him, voiceless, down
Among sharp-tongued reeds by the stream,
    His misshape
Darting there, trebled in the current's
    Shiftings, a swimmer

And her two sisters, who mocked him.
Where, I thought to cry, but could not,
    So I may give praise
Rightly, is the greater craftsman
    Who has made beauty

At such remove that my desire
Is coarsened, a love of form, illumined
    In that shimmering
As theft, and I am driven down
    With Alberich,

Squat, sputtering in the foam,
While about him the scattered glare
    Gathers, a drift
Of river-mottled gold. Poor handiwork,
    He thrashed the shallows,

As the swimmers chanted, spray
At the bounds of his reflection.
    Bitter, renouncing
Such fellowship, I walked out at dawn
    Where all night

Rain had fallen, freezing on the snow,
And as wind struck the orchard,
    Laughter rose
Around me among the dying branches,
    Glitterings of shape

Flown. Dazzled, slipping,
I grasped for balance an apple bough,
    Which splintered, unequal
To loveliness, to sympathy, diminished
    And so my equal.

Cedar Shoals

If I had wanted for a long time to find—
    In a field north of Troy,
New York, or near the Seneca's ruined castle
    At Boughton Hill, or deep-
Set among the glacial shards, the kettle holes
    And drumlins of Mendon—
A pond of sweet water and its source, a creek
    Still sweeter and bitter
Cold, a vein of iron ore red in the bedrock,
    And a cairn of fieldstones
Reflected; if I had hoped to kneel at last
    On fallen cattails, drink
And be absolved of my pettiness, minor
    Fears, minor affections,
I might tell this more simply. That night I thought
    I wanted nothing, just
To drive to a party just outside Lone Tree
    And to find there friends, books,
Gossip about friends and books. I missed my turn
    And drove miles through those fields
On oiled-stone roads, dirt roads, ruts. I was so lost
    I tried to calm myself
With Whitman, lines I remembered—*A Child said*
    What is the grass? fetching
It to me with full hands. How could I answer . . .
    And how could I answer,
Who saw no *uniform hieroglyphic*, but
    Dry, wintry stalks, dead leaves?
Listen, I thought my life might go on simply,
    Not as grass spears glossing
A graveyard sermon, not as thistle-blow, not
    The night shine of marsh gas,

The endless passion of a cow's four stomachs,
	But with the scudding, failing
Rhythm of farm-road junctions, with the slight, finite,
	Forgetful, untouched light
Of the gas gauge. Just where the washboard road swung
	Down hard, and the tires bucked
On scree and rain-scored clay the color of raw iron,
	I saw the coyote
Break from corn stubble and lope along the track
	Of what was not a road,
Not even a barn lane, but the near-vanished
	Slough of a railway spur:
Cinders, ties rotting to ground. And then the truck swerved,
	Shimmied, caught on old rails.
I had turned off without thinking, following
	What? The moonlight was scaled,
Blue-tinged, slick as on fast water on his scruff,
	And in his mouth, the haunch,
Raw-fleshed, of some farm creature caught the same sheen,
	Rippling, spring-harsh, spilling
Over the right-of-way, over the wild sprigs
	Of winter wheat, over
The scavenger, his meal, my hand on the shift,
	Granting even the torn
Planks of the rail bed a boundless, shifting life.
	The coyote struck off
Where the embankment rose so fast I couldn't turn,
	And then I saw the bridge,
An iron double-span above the Cedar River,
	Drove between the pitted
Girders, while below the rapids curdled, squalled.
	It was like those long dreams

In which sleep becomes a death: all the quickened
    Elements reclaiming
Their first, material allegiances—dirt
    On the windshield gone thick
With spray; the ignition spark rocking, homeless,
    Charge to discharge on the dial;
The moon-struck air trembling, splintered, in the fits
    Of the bridge struts, darkened;
The sour lyric of fast water. Then no sound.
    On the far bank, the truck
Stalled, and just in front of me the palisades,
    Granite cliff faces torn
Like mud in a drought stream bed: washouts, fissures,
    Broken veins of ore, faults,
All intersecting like the endless chisel
    Lines of some character
Defeated by the chaos of a dead language,
    The character for chaos
Or defeat. How can I tell you what I felt then,
    When I had lost myself
In that trace of spirit—fleet, unspent, common—
    And found at last nothing
More than insistent, untranslatable stone.
    Once, in Spain, hitchhiking,
I was picked up by the *Guardia Civil*;
    One held my passport, mouthed
As if he were dumb the foreign syllables,
    Raised his machine pistol,
Then threw down my papers, spat, and turned away
    Just as indifferently
As I'd shrugged aside street beggars in Madrid.
    He couldn't even say my name.

To keep from staring at his gun, I counted
  The three teeth he had left,
Three stubs etched with the same absence as the cliffs,
  Absence of . . . *We're dead men,*
I thought, *who walk without sympathy, who walk*
  Dressed in our shrouds. Again,
Whitman, his hard-urged words, urged in denial
  Of what lies so deep in
Longing and grief, is so unanswerable,
  It filled my mouth like stone.
Could I answer, with him, *the smallest sprout shows*
  There is really no death,
When I had not found I could believe, only
  That I longed to?
                    Listen,
If I said such desire seems a kind of love,
  Would you take that on faith,
Or want to? I sat by those cliffs a long time.

2

Fragment

Out from the New York Central tracks,
Above a cast-iron tier of steps, rust-diminished,
Scaling from the embankment, crying
In midair a kingfisher dives, white at his throat,

White slash of water where the great herons wade.
What is the beauty as they rise, ungainly,
From the ruined Hudson, what beauty
In the stiff, broken spine of the needlefish drifting

Against tarred pilings along the valley road to NYC,
Where nothing is left fragile or whole?
At the last turnstile, when Orpheus
Faltered in that passage of guttered, transient souls,

What candor, irreducible
Under the weft of her flesh, loosening then, leaf mold,
Would he not trust to memory, muse
Who kept so faithfully the glint of sun on the fur of beasts,

The ripened tenor of vine leaves in midsummer,
Which were his song. He turned, liar,
To seize the unstrung tendons, the mode of elegy
And rote, mode of the perishable,

Descending.

The Hudson at Mechanicville

Below the Chesapeake & Ohio's
   Tanker cars stalled mid-
      Span on an iron trestle,
The sun has joined a barge
   To glory on the water.
      Hawsers slack, a load
Of gravel, barrels,
   She swings lordly, gently
      Across the Hudson
From a mill they are tearing down,
   Four great brick stacks
      And a tumbled furnace.
In fidelity, in Schenectady,
   Between St. Anthony's
      And the Alps Grill,
I have kept my devotions
   To the second-floor window
      Of a duplex, where one day
A man leaned out, mouthed
   Over some litany,
      Swept his arm, in blessing
Or not
   Across the railroad bridge
      And the line of commuters' cars
On Nott Street.
   But this was nothing
      So human, the Hudson
A foundry of untempered light,
   The barge riding in brilliance,
      In chaos, beyond the heap

Of fallen brick, except
>For a washbowl of yellow
>>Porcelain on a broken,
Blue-tiled wall. Hard used
>And lost to use,
>>It hung three stories up
In clarity, in the tremor
>Of the wreckers' crane,
>>And did not fall, while
The men clearing the lot
>Of glass and tile hefted
>>Shovelfuls of glazed
Shards, which flared and altered
>Nothing of their long expense
>>Of labor past sunset,
The river a dark blue drift
>Of smoke, where two scows
>>Were moored, and the shadows
Of the loading crew bent
>And lifted, weighted with the grace
>>Of presence in such transience.

Auriesville

This failing month in haze,
Still the passion of the leaves
Sharp-tongued in flame, then risen,
Their acrid communion caught
Like held breath in my throat.
Along Route 20, troopers
Check the hunters' kill,
And roadhouse parking lots
Fill with men in blaze
And khaki. One fine buck hung
Gutshot from a tow hook,
And a boy in camouflage
Gripped each far tip of horn,
Laughed, reloaded, vanished
Among the dun red maples.
What spares us from a world
Turned to the pitiless
Reflection of the self,
If not the body's dumb,
Broken testimony?
Before Auriesville, I parked
At the martyrs' shrine
Where the Jesuit father Jogue,
Caught in the Mohawks' grave,
Offended love of order,
Knelt at the gauntlet, cried
Behold the narrow way
To Paradise, and so
Denied what fellowship
His suffering might claim.
A leaf in flame, my car
Shook in a rising wind,

And as a prayer I sought
The commonality
Of loss, that pure attention,
As if a hunter stood
Before his buck, the horned
Head slack against the hoist,
And could not speak, witness
At the perishing of will.

Mandolin

Because the Byrds were on his car
Radio singing *My Back Pages,*
My friend remembered the guitar
He smashed before he dove off stage

Into the crowd of high school faces
He hated. "Jerks and small-town jocks
In letter jackets, their straight-laced
Cheerleader promqueen dates. We wrecked

Two amps that night to get good loving,
Respect. What else did we want then?
I turned and watched our drummer shove
His set right off the risers, spun

And tossed my Fender at the speakers.
So much for all the crap I took
From coaches, teachers, north-side greasers,
Anyone who didn't like my looks."

He shifted into third, too hard.
"So who cares now. I graduated,
Couldn't afford a new guitar.
Soon all the songs I knew were dated."

"Yeah," I said, "I made gigs too,
Played trumpet on those call-and-answer
Riffs in a blue-eyed soul review,
Sweet licks to draw the couples closer

Across the free-throw line, our spot
Dim for the last dance, slow fade. . . .
But I wanted to move them, not
Just help some local hood get laid.

You know what I was like? Long-haired,
Too hip to smile, jeans always torn,
Nervous around adults, a spare
Joint in the case under my horn."

"Shut up," he said. "You're thirty-four,
I'm older. Why should we still care
Who put us down, or what we wore
Or were?" He let me out. Upstairs

I turned the radio on to static,
Off, picked up the mandolin
I found in my grandmother's attic
Cupboard, forgotten, with her pin

(A nickel silver lyre and stave)
And portrait of the Norwich Girls'
Mandolin Orchestra. Too grave
For such a kid, her fingers curled

On the neck, she stared, not at the glint
Of studio light on the lens,
But toward the frame, at the thumbprint's
Brownish whorl, as if she sensed

How she would hold the picture, bend
Years later toward a self so fast
Receding it seemed all ornament,
Soft grace note, nothing more. Past

Mending, I thought, when I undid
The cloth case, found the neck unstrung,
The pegs frozen. But she'd just died,
My first death, and it seemed wrong

Not to try some elegy,
So I tinkered, got it fixed, then lied
And said I practiced. Finicky
To tune, sweet toned, no amplified

Harsh declaration of the self,
It asked such delicacy. Four years
Ago I took it off the shelf,
Restrung it again, oiled the gears,

Because I'd dreamt I was that boy
Who didn't dance, stood near the speakers,
Forgot the concert band for Sly
Stone's trumpet charts, new sneakers

For black boots and a leather jacket.
In the dark gym, I saw my face
As grave, intent as hers, but lacking
In my unease all her grace.

An older man watched from the bleachers.
He kept his tweed coat buttoned, frowned,
And checked his watch. A coach, a teacher—
I couldn't place him—a chaperone?

Out in the emptying parking lot,
He stared into the rearview mirror,
Uncertain, as if he forgot
What it was that brought him there.

Hands in pockets, I was too nervous
To ask his name, and turned my back
As if indifferent or embarrassed.
I woke to the echo of a sax

And trumpet when the last chord dies,
Trembling as on a mandolin's
Twin strings, sustained, not quite on key . . .
Like my friend's anger or my own

Memory that loiters, shy,
Among the lunch lines, lockers, amps,
Unsure what I wanted or why
I still don't think I've got it. I damped

The strings, retuned, and tried to sound
The triplets of a jig. Not yet.
Again. My fingers faltered, found,
Then broke time on the narrow frets.

A Theater Song for Kurt Weill

Because we are poor and cannot dance
    A tango through the garden,
Not knowing the steps as you do, lacking
    Leisure or inclination

To learn them properly, because
    Our debts, distracting, slow
Our lean pursuit of credit,
    Because the *thus* and *so*

Of pleas, waivers, applications
    Is not our native tongue—
A dialect untranslatable
    Except by those whom Hunger,

Our great patron, has inspired,
    Rounding their bellies tight
So all may read his signs and wonder—
    Because we cannot buy

Or sell or dance and are refused
    And go with a good riddance,
We have come to Silverlake
    Where nothing is forbidden.

    Where nothing is forbidden,
        And there is always a surplus.
    Where Hunger is our patron,
        His bounty is our profit.

Where nothing is forbidden us,
    Except to fill our bellies,
For Hunger guided us to this place.
    His breath darkened the water

Like tarnish on a spoon. At his cry
    Need flared in us like torches,
And in that fury we saw the shanties
    Reflected along the shoreline

Blaze, a sparking, tangled net
    Of taverns, brothels, shambles,
A raging commerce, where our poor flesh
    Was all the capital ventured.

Struck with greed, we staggered, lost
    Our footing in the marshlands,
While the town fires wavered beyond our grasp,
    Bright oil on the water.

Some clawed at waves, others swore,
    Stole bread, a neighbor's daughter,
Or barricaded the shanty doors.
    So Silverlake was founded.

    So Silverlake was founded
        To teach this lesson: truly,
    If the poor feed on each other,
        They will feast and still go hungry.

So Silverlake was founded, sir,
    And christened the next morning
When we awoke and found—no city
    Of butchery, whoring, burning—

Only mist rising with the dawn
    Over water as sleek as you are,
And polished like your table service.
    We knelt down by the shore,

Thirsting to see our reflections drenched,
    Brilliant, in that vast splendor.
Nothing. The lake's unwavering gaze,
    Expansive, placid, candid,

Held no acknowledgment of us.
    And then, a sudden, consuming
Glare of sunlight, a dismissal,
    Enraged, of our presumption

To hope that we might share such wealth.
    Blinded, we called that night
Our own. And we are not ungrateful.
    No we are not ungrateful

> *To learn how fleeting light is,*
> > *Nor would we barter our plateful*
> *Of craving for such transience,*
> > *For we are always with you.*

At Arnold's Monument

On Bemis Heights, a scant
Noon haze has scoured the blunt
Hills across the Hudson
As blank as chalk. Undone,

Paine's rhetoric and Franklin's
Industry—the twined
Barbed wire of these poor farms,
Fields dull and uniform

In March, tenants gone
After betrayal, sudden
And long-prepared. Their yards
One morning filled with cars

For auction of the mattress
Springs, the tools, the dresser,
A sprawl of plain goods piled
Out in plain sight. Arnold

Knew British pounds might dress
His Loyalist wife. Relentless,
He desired honor
And its perquisites, a warrior's

Pension, quick preferment.
He knew his own worth, spent
Generously his worn,
Stubborn forces to turn

Burgoyne at Freeman's farm,
Kept his accounts with care.
What recompense for two
Wounds in his leg, for proof

That his superiors—Schuyler,
Gates—were timid, idle,
As he was not? Nothing,
Neither rank nor profit.

He turned at last to England
And so is less forgotten
Than those, fainter, more worthy,
Who refused him. Just north

In Saratoga Springs,
The robber barons thinned
Their pettish accidie
A little in the tepid

Alkaline baths and, healed,
Played stocks and horses, dealt
Themselves another, finer
Hand. He was their kind,

Bitter in denial, faithless
But to self-interest.
On Bemis Heights, the wind's
Anthem of spent limbs,

Fierce, tangled purposes,
Rises with the haze
Above the fallen barns,
Above the cavalryman's

Marble boot. No name
Is carved there in his praise,
Whose legacy persists
In all this emptiness.

Days of 1974

This poem began in honor
Of all that is as sure, common, persistent
    As the talc-fine ochre dust
That rose behind my Fiat on the hill roads
    Between Naples and Penn Yann

That year when I first loved you. We drove so far
    That the scaling porch shingles
And cupolas of failed towns, the ramshackle
    Docks, bait shops, day-sailors' bars,
Were lost in vineyard lanes, terraced vines,

    In glinting, rough-fleshed grape leaves.
Then, at evening, the stuttering neon
    Of old hotels, the taprooms,
Their plank booths and tar-brick walls, bright oil traces
    From some fisherman's outboard,

All the casual, local trash we drove back to . . .
    I remember everything.
You knelt, where the latticed afternoon light scored
    The broken loft floor, to pick
From a heap of baling wire and scrap lumber

    A splintered tongue of blue glass,
An etched design of hop blooms, their stalks braided,
    From a patent nostrum flask.
And that fall, in the Cottage Hotel's cheap bar—
    Where I'd watched two shift workers

Smash glasses, dodge and scrap, because a woman
    In boots and a worn silk shawl
Would rather dance alone while the string band played
    Sugar Hill—waiting for you,
I traced the carvings on my booth: phone numbers,

    Hearts and moons, propositions
To no one, hair twisted like vines, signatures
    Of impatience and rough awe.
Tell me, how did we pass so easily all
    The stern, thirsty, late nights,

The early mornings, bright frost, the blue-struck dawn
    In our uncurtained window?
Just at last call, you walked in, led me—still drunk,
    Singing *Sail Away Ladies*—
Into the first snow. And, our car fishtailing,

    The headlamps lighting nothing
But stubbled, drifting fields, we passed a storefront
    On West Lake Road, and I stopped
And saw, between the lures and bait cans, the pin-up
    Calendars and trolling rods,

Our reflections, huddled on the leaded glass,
    Flushed with the one beer sign
Still lit, so far off-season. So I would praise
    Anything—that sad marsh smell,
The cans and cigarette stubs by the boat launch,

The Depression farmhouses
On Sunnyside, bleached, abandoned—anything
    Offered in memory of
A good drive home, days as common, sure as dust,
    As snow, and as persistent.

Burnt Hills

Because I tired of words that were not acts,
I thought to bow to the rust-burnt
Veins of a maple leaf broken in the driveway,
Graveled trace of the sweet,
Unarguable concentration of sugar on the tongue—
All I hoped to become, leaving
As dross a husk,

Blazing. Instead I have signed
A thirty-year note for payment, taking on credit
The deed to a house between two orchards
And the Baptists' graveyard. There's nothing,
Said a friend who helped me move,
Like a mortgage
To bring your mortality home.

Among the furnishings of her family and mine,
It is not loss I tell
Over to myself, but ignorance. I do not know
Whose labor wore the wheel's treadle,
Or who named this town, or why.
The first settlers came from Stillwater on the Hudson,
Ten miles east or so,
A short haul to come to so desolate a name.

And because I cannot understand what moved them
If not words, I imagine them silent
Among candles in the unshingled frame of their church.
Through the hewn beams, in the evening haze,
The hills are tangled with second growth
They've not yet laid an axe to.
If the moon is a sickle then, if it is full

Silver or burnished red in autumn,
They are praying for whatever I would ask for:
Not to live beyond the given term, not for the sheaves
Only, but for the emptiness of a field in November,
For the bled veins of the maple
And the commingling of fire, branch-wood, sap,
In sweetness on the tongue.

Letter to Adrian Frazier

On the East Stoney, the riffle's dance
Drags my fly beyond resemblance
To anything. Below a bridge
That joined the lost town to a ledge
Of ore that didn't pay, no trout
Are rising. I might as well get out,
But wade to slacker water, cast,
Lured still to see in the stream a test

Of an imitative craft.
Late last night, the loon's drawn laugh
Quavered from the narrow lake.
I took my notebook, stayed awake,
Tried to catch that native trill,
But notes of longing, pride, bereavement,
Tumbled in a tangled current
Unsounded by my syllables.

So I quit, took out the book you gave,
Derek Mahon's *Poems.* I know you love
The Irish poets, their verse letters
Where a musician's faith in meter
Requires no great departure from
What we pursue, the idiom.
Take Mahon, how his couplets turn
Tartan toughs, Dante, Danish porn,

Botticelli, stormy weather, Joyce,
To urgencies of a quiet voice,
Still faithful to the civic desire
For civil speech—no razor wire,

Barricades, or bomber's caustic
Inflammatory rhetoric,
But a truce, where irony, self-doubt,
Are rendered as clarity of thought.

I read and couldn't understand
How he found such grace in a torn land,
While we founder on this unspoken
Truth: in America what's broken
Is all that's beautiful. The Hudson,
The Kaydeross, the Battenkill,
Think how those rivers find their sudden
Picturesque power near empty mills:

In shadows of the burnt-out stacks,
A stippled, bright trail blazed with wrecks.
Adrian, if memory's our muse,
Her stock in trade is scrap, and those
Who find, in refuse, refusal's firm
"I am" may forge a fragmentary
Art that recovers the ordinary,
The local, but only on terms

As singular as they are exclusive
Of those lacking the stubborn, useful,
Ungainly grace of Williams' Elsie,
Those whom no poem saves. I see
Them close up on the late night news,
Conmen, convicts, the born-to-lose,
Crazy, pure American
Products. One drifter filled his van

With guns, grenades. Because he listened
In his all-white church to the preacher's lesson
Of armageddon and the antichrist—
Whose servants stand among the just
In subways, lines for food stamps,
Ask for change, set up their camps
In packing crates on gutted lots—
He kept his pistol loaded, shot

A black state trooper who flagged him down,
Then told the jury how he found
A new life, born again. They listened,
His language as much theirs as Whitman's,
Henry Thoreau's or Herman Melville's,
A local dialect that dwells
Below the yawp, rage for a pure
Privacy or at the poor

Shoddiness of appearances,
In fierce denial that circumstances,
Tattered, accidental, cruel,
Are all the self has to reveal.
I pull my spent fly from the spray,
Hackles sheared, fur gone, the gray
Thread dangling from the hook, which slips,
Draws blood. High noon. High time to quit.

Below the falls, the Stoney's roily
Passage dwindles, like a story
That wanders, inconclusive, grieved,
The teller's face a half-drowned leaf.

In early spring, I heard a neighbor
Say, "I wasn't lost or winded,
No middle-aged man in a stupor
Of will where dark trees form a line.

New snow had fallen in the woods,
And then a glaze of rain. I stood
In the splendid labyrinth perception
Becomes, or so says Emerson,
Where there's no god to interfere
With our exile in the shattered mirror
Of mere experience. A buck
Had cracked the crust. I crossed his tracks

Three times before I knew I'd circled
For an hour or more, I was so dazzled.
I came out where the shale-banked hills
Fall scrabbly to the Alplaus Kill,
A mile from home. The sun was low,
But what I saw was not a sunset's
Romance of violet and russet.
Like kindled air, light caught the snow

And flared. Below me on the creek,
A glare so sharp it left me weak-
Kneed, shaking as if with hunger,
Breathless—a boy who'd skipped his supper,
Run miles to sit above his town
And watch the evening lights come on.
The city I saw, bright on the ice,
Was the unbounded trope of place,

American, sublime, whose center,
All periphery, was nowhere.
The sun lowered. The twilit snow
Was as grainy as a newsprint photo,
And in the gorge the tree limbs, tumbled
Shale, a charcoal scrawl of rubble,
The garbled, incoherent plea
Of disorder for sympathy.

I thought then of that desert suburb
Where mannikins posed undisturbed
Around their ranch-house dinner tables,
A scene out of *Leave It to Beaver*,
Until the bomb test hit, a fever
Wind that bent their yard trees double.
Where the cliff dropped off, I sat
And watched the whole sky turn to slate.

Below me on black ice the moon
Fractured like a vase on stone,
A sudden pointillistic flourish,
Auroral, shimmering, which vanished
As quickly as my city's cut-
Glass changed in memory to what
Seemed a Doré etching of hell,
More touching, more believable,

More certain than any paradise
That is not lost, its flickering trace
Like specks of mica on a road,
Sparkling, scattered hints of ore,

Ungatherable, pure, fool's gold."
He stopped then, sank back in his chair,
While out on the lake a loon
Began his cry. Later, alone,

I knew that I had come to see
This country "in isolate flecks,"
As Williams said, searching the dreck
For something broken to let be.
Now that I've packed away my reel
And rod, the bronze-red brookies rise,
Breaking the surface of the pool
After a hatch of dappled flies

And churn the water with their rippling,
Purposeful hunger for the trembling
Flight of the ephemeral,
Water and fish joined in the swirling
Sign of a rage that seeks no order
Apart from the quickening currents where,
I thought as I walked to the car,
What we love breaks on what we are.

3

The Star Chamber

When the guides put out their lamps,
All but one—low-wicked, close-shaded, intimate—
Emerson, in the Star Chamber, in the great
    Sprawling grasp of Mammoth Cave,

Thought this singular light no
More striking than Lydian's hand at dusk, pale silk
Across his forehead. A sheen, but no true light.
    In that rich, insistent air,

He could not draw a sure breath,
And wished he might loosen his collar, shake off
With his stiff coat the sudden, quickening trace
    Of closeness. The lamp sputtered,

And then darkness—a body
Without depth or significance, offering
No purchase to his will. His boot shied on milk-
    Fleshed limestone, and he fell. Chilled,

Dull, when the lamp was relit,
Then trimmed still lower, he had not faith enough
To grasp his friend's hand, finding his own so numb.
    It was not as if he dreamt,

But as if he fell deep in
Nature's dream: all men still in utter worship,
Like the Indian, lost in the cavern, who crouched
    Beside a gravel slide, head

Bent as if in reverence,
And became a natural thing—no man. Stars—
How had they appeared above him?—came forward
     In procession, no longer

     His sure, interpretable
Figures of great desire: no Andromache
Straining from her rock, no Perseus to solve
     The stubborn indwelling of stone,

     But uninhabited sky,
Sublime! He ached for it. One of the party
Began to sing—*Oh beautiful star*—but he
     Neither joined in the chorus

     Nor could discern in the vast,
Brightening heaven that stark and clear melody
He took to be his own. Wavering, helpless
     To encompass or to stand

     Apart from this deep-sprung swell,
Which was the cavern's gift—the body like fire-
Struck air, yet his body still—he felt such joy.
     Later, on a lecture tour,

     He named the cave's offering
Illusion, and praised those men who see through all
Embraces, yet are no celibates. Later.
     The lamps flared. He stood like stone.

Remains

For once I would speak plainly
About what I have loved well,
     The buckling masonry
Of a wireless factory abandoned to a field
     Of blue chicory and wild carrot,
          Bramble-ridden.

But how can I tell you simply
About what no longer remains even
     In memory
Without qualification? Finches start,
     Gold, from the roadside,
          And tangles of fox grape

Engage the grayish mortar. Nothing speaks
Of the stillness in the scattered
     Shade of the rafters.
Only a shrilling of crickets and peepers,
     And the redwings
          Crying from the marsh,

Flushing and darting—what peace
Could I have taken from these,
     Or from the reddish bloom
Of sumac clustered on emptying boughs,
     Brush of late grass,
          Dry shudderings of reeds?

All September, as the maples
Blazed, grew mottled, as brittle as rust,
     I read in Jung

Of the alchemist's *nigredo*, opus
　　Of corroding fires,
　　　　Thought fallen

Into the smoldering of damp leaves.
On a dogeared page, Mercurius,
　　Guide of souls,
Lay bound, his spirit flown, a raven
　　Spinning upward, his cry harsh,
　　　　Unwitting,

Nothing to draw the drifting stars
From dispersal inward, into certain
　　Brilliance, into song.
Above the barn, Orion rose, mute
　　Club-handed figure
　　　　Of unknowing,

As I worked under the trouble light
On the truck's dead ignition. Lost
　　To my own anger
At the drift of things, winter
　　Like white ash
　　　　Across the unmown fields,

I walked to that factory, and any peace
That comes with the thought of it
　　Is in the act of memory—
Not what memory holds, but an offering
　　In thanks that I have passed
　　　　A misspent season.

Elegy as a Triplet of
Three-lobed Leaves

I know a maple tree
In a field of second growth
That I would dedicate
To a memory like wind
Within the hollow trunk,
A cry of sweetness, native
And bitter in elegy.

Not the Vermont & Northern's
Long whistle at the grade
Crossing, which is money
In someone's pocket, not
The slow-drawn shrilling cry
Of frozen boxcar couplers
Drowning the road crew's talk.

But wind, blown through the stained
Iron girders of a bridge
Where two boys smoke, their throats
As raw as the hands of fathers
They love and run from and
Will be, caught in the broken
Calendar of the swing shift.

     *   *   *

My roommate knew by heart
A poem about Ohio
Where on the high school fields
Boys break against each other
In honor of what their fathers
Mortgaged, pride or kindness.
How had we grown so soon so

Sure we were our fathers'
Slim odds? In Danny's Rock
We'd watch the morning drinkers
Around the horseshoe bar,
Faces a long time fallen
From any family album.
None of them was the father

Who earned my keep, who'd earned
More than the poems I botched
That year. His silences
After a day's work blew
Through them, like new snow
In a field I walked with nothing
To turn my hand against.

*   *   *

This elegy is for
A country where our fathers
Are driven through factories,
Trick work, office blocks,
Driven like wind through sere
Branches in poems of sons

Who have learned that no song
Restores the bough to leaf.
At twilight in the drifting
Snow on Blue Barns Road,
A great buck grazed my fender,
Stumbled down the rail bed.
Under a hollow maple,

His muzzle gray, his gut
Tight from a starving winter,
He reared and faltered, spun
Into brush. And I was left
With what remains when spirit
Is pared away like words
In wind. What's left is wind.

Country Blues

In the fire department band, I played
For free beer and
Five bucks a night in small-time
Carnival parades
In little towns where only the funeral homes
Keep up, and the old hotels
Are taprooms now, with music on the weekends.

From our suburbs,
Bob and I would drive in the red pickup
His father used, summers,
On the Vineyard,
Along those secondary country roads,
Through orchards
And tumble-down poor-dirt farms.

In the shade of the blistered walls
Of the migrant camp
On a scrub lot beside the canning plant,
Empty between harvests,
We'd argue bands or politics,
Or watch a kid in leather,
Engineer boots, a feedstore hat,

Jack up the rear end of his Fury
To gun past us, another night,
Where the Ridge Road stretched for miles along the lake.
All week I practiced
The trumpet fingerings to *Washington Post*
And *The Stars and Stripes Forever*
On the silver Beuscher

My father bought for nothing in the thirties.
American Patrol, Hands Across the Sea,
The runs and trills of more confident years
Skirled between pizza joints and laundromats
As we trailed a color guard
Of girl scouts and the ladies' auxiliary
Past the mayor and the old men

Waiting in uniforms, wheelchairs,
At the reviewing stand
On the steps of the VFW hall.
In memory, all those nights
Blur into rain on the windshield, lights
Sputtering along the midway
As we marched through drizzle and a cold wind.

It was the last carnival that year,
And we talked too long
About how we'd leave, for schools, for good.
Past the generators,
The carnies smoking in a circle,
The closed-up 4-H booths and sausage stands,
I thought, a little drunk, I'd play

One last fight strain to the still orchards
And raised my horn, took breath.
His hand swollen, scraped
At the knuckles, creased with oil and primer paint,
He grabbed my arm, a kid
In a black T-shirt, long hair tied back.
His denim vest was loose

Around the shoulders of the girl beside him,
Who shivered, clutched herself,
Like someone spinning off on the ferris wheel,
But holding on, barely
Holding on.
"Give me the horn," he said,
"I've got no money, but I can get some.

I've never seen a horn like that."
She leaned against him. "Just let him hold it,
Just hold it a minute.
What money could he get?"
As the headlights of a van
Picked us out, slurred away on that country road,
I saw his mouth was bruised

From a fight, a fall,
But he took my horn, blew
One garbled note, slow, after another
Across the emptying midway,
The junked Chevies and Fords
Hauled away from the demolition race that afternoon,
Some country blues.

Lucky Seven

In a nearly empty off-season café, just across
From the row of grand Saratoga hotels, I lost faith
In the elegance of the facades fronting Congress Park,
Their flush, hardly graceful nineties air—restored, privileged
Moments of an assured, more frankly reserved century.
It wasn't the desk clerk in the gently inflected dusk
Of the old Adelphi's mirror-and-mahogany lobby,
Who told me luncheon was served only during the season.
He looked me over and thought I might do, in the season.
It wasn't NY 32 North, where the Hudson's one long
Iron-colored millrace for Mechanicville, Stillwater, Troy,
Those stalled factory towns, or the detour in Cohoes
Past what was left of a warehouse some kid torched the
    night before,
To a dark block of turn-of-the-century row houses
Where the wage hands lived, houses of fieldstone, coarse
    masonry—
Tiny, vacant, shelving downhill toward the stream and the
    mills.
It wasn't that, but how I'd imagined Saratoga
As a story out of James, a parable of urban
Restoration—someone's life, so much conventional scrap,
Wrought with delicate, tempered irony toward a flourish
Of pure character, as slight and certain as the pen stroke
Of William H. (Public Be Damned) Vanderbilt's business
    hand.
I'd driven so far, parked beside the public mineral spring—
Where two women, shabby, old enough to invest what faith
Remained to them in the healing virtues of hard water,
Filled plastic jugs at the tap—to find my way through a
    draft
I could not finish, a long, epistolary story,

Which came to me as suddenly as the erratics rise
On Adirondack hillsides, those great metamorphic shards
Of glacial drift and turn, as immanent as memory
When memory fails: a huge stone shadowing the pathway,
Figurations of lichen, scars and glyphs of shifting ground,
And at its foot, in the duff of pine needles and bracken,
Between lesser boulders, an entrance too small for passage.
I was recalling a quarrel with my father, about—
I couldn't recall, but he had lost his job that year,
And we could just afford the cabin we'd always taken,
An old hunters' camp from the Depression, lath and
    clapboard,
Blistered paint, a dock of splitting, creosote-soaked pilings,
At the end of a packed dirt road, where the land swelled
In a tumble of weathered spruce and ore-streaked granite
    spurs.
I was so angry with him that I ran without speaking,
Following the hill's shoulder on a rutted logging road
That vanished in a thicket of scrub growth—young saplings
Tangled with heavy, splintered trunks, windfalls from a
    hurricane,
Bleached as dull as marrow. I traced that chaos of crossed
    paths,
Until I lost all direction but what the storm's wreck left
And came, swearing, my hands stained with pitch, bruised
    as from a brawl,
To a pillared wall of stone, fissures like steps on its face.
At its crest, there was a hollow in the rock, worn by rain
Into a vessel for a dozen tiny skeletons
Scattered just below the rim. A cry—half-hiss, half-keening—
Rose from a cairn of loose stone as I bent to touch those
    bones,

And a weasel sprang out, reddish, swollen, spitting with rage
That lashed his limbs like a sudden wind. Shaken, I slipped,
    rolled
Down along bare rock that led nowhere but to a cliff's edge.
Below me was the calm sheen of a mountain lake at noon—
Bright glare on the horizon, and the stones and branching
    snags
Clear in the shallow bay, my path's snarled, downfallen
    pattern
Distanced, altered by the tannic stain of the lake water
Into the reflective silence of a daguerreotype.
Bracing myself, I turned and saw on an arm of the cove
The great unbarked beams of the lodge, the trellis of pine
    boughs
With a wild rose blooming there, windows of brown and
    green tint,
The gazebo on an island just off shore, gabled roofs,
All doubled in the brilliance of the lake, as if nature
Had found its quietus there in artifice, a final
Perfect stillness of form, a grace of reticence and calm
For which I'd renounce anything and call myself lucky.
It was out of that stillness that the other story came.
I'd written the first letter, from a young divinity
Candidate. Bostonian, brash, more stunned than he admits
By Saratoga's gracious, barely proper elegance,
He advances a month's parish fees for the smallest room
In the Grand Union Hotel, unpacks his decent, well-worn
Evening suit, stares at lines of washing in the courtyard,
Hesitates between hotel stationery and his own,
Writes at last, beneath the embossed seal of the
    management,
His hometown pastor and adviser, explaining his choice

For the retreat customary before an ordination
By pleading that here, between the marble busts, sporting
    prints,
And racing dailies, he'll meet his future parishioners,
Men of leisure and affairs and their wives, and so begin
The work of his ministry by turning their thoughts from
    odds
On the nearest filly, tea with some distant connection
Of the Morgans, the Durants, to less temporal concerns.
"Sir, how goes it with your soul?" he asks them all, bears
    their snubs
With breezy, unembarrassed grace. So far it was easy
Writing, the boy's uncertain, tireless, assumed worldliness
Betraying with every turn of pious phrase how less grand
Than wealth his own vocation seemed. But I balked at the
    postscript,
Where, dimming the gaslit rooms, the ornamental crystal,
Glint of tips on gold-flecked trays, a sudden American
Chiaroscuro would temper the style, as if a genre
Painting of a racing day and crowds, all expansive sky,
Had been rubbed away, leaving tangled pine limbs, erratics,
The hard Adirondack twilight. But where, in Congress Park,
Or on Broadway between the tack shop and the ice-cream
    stand,
Would I catch a glimpse of him, the figure in evening dress
On the stairwell, a sprig of hemlock in his lapel,
Who tempts the student away from his prayer and solitaire,
To dine in a suite reserved year-round, Waterford and Sèvres
Bright on the table, an oval flask on a cut-glass tray,
The servants well trained, discreet, as poised and groomed
    as horseflesh?
And where would I find his voice, or his stale nobility

Of manner, his quick flare of self-possession over brandy?
The scrolls and turrets of the mansions were no help at all,
But later, in the café lined with worn prints of the town,
I found, in a dark frame at the end of the bar, a map
Of the old Adirondacks—stage routes, narrow-gauge
  railroads,
Spider-lined filigree of tourist wealth, and at its heart
The creased, brownish mountains where I'd lost myself in
  anger.
I sought him then, not as I had hoped to, in elegance
Of vision, in eloquence, but in a tale recited
As if against his will, his voice hushed, burred, retold later
In the student's suddenly unsteady hand: *As a boy,*
In thick spring, on an island where his family's great lodge
Was built wing by wing with gains in futures, in pork, in
  grains,
He heard his father cry out that hell's remembered in red
Veins of granite on the cliff's torn face, that leaf mold
  sinking
In the shallows, blue-sulphur dragonflies, spinning, mating,
Above lakes as rough as moss-worn tablets in a churchyard,
Are the backing of the world's trembling mirror, a ground
  of self
Lost. Saw that poor madman hanging in the pine rafters,
  saw God
Tangled in the blackberries and blowdowns, the great raw
  slides
Of Owlshead Mountain. Dear sir . . . But as I walked out
  again
Past the old spa, past the park, I could not convince myself
That a tale heard as dimly as a sigh through the strange,
  sharp

Ring of brandy, through lamplight, was what shook the
    student so.
Perhaps he sensed some falseness in the telling, and soon
    all
Saratoga seemed nothing but a mirror, dim and blank,
But for its single desire: to frame, in the pretension
Of candor, an exclusive, tempting, cloying world—nothing
Lasting in reflection there that was not touched with silver.
Lost in the story's deadfalls, the handsome, easy pathos
Of a wealthy man, the soul of self-reliance, wounded
To the soul by nature's text, how could the boy see clearly
Who had told him this: the son who, surviving, learned by
    heart
What glass most surely holds the spirit's fluid, volatile
    light—
A brandy goblet, hand-blown, edged with gold, held lightly
    but
With certainty, as if such richness were a trust, fragile,
Against all mere gravity. It was not as I had imagined it,
A fable of callow pride, humbled, rededicated.
No, the boy would wander, dazed, small figure in the sepia-
Tint prints of the gilded age on the wall of the café,
Drawn always toward those fine resorts he couldn't truly
    afford.
And his host would lift his drink again, turn it in the light,
Find nothing but his own troubled reflection in the glass.
Across the street, men in rope slings dangled on the brick
    front
Of the Adelphi Hotel, scraping the old trim, swinging
Below the gold-edged sign. I knew the story had no end
That I could find in Saratoga, a town no less false
Or candid than a robber baron's homemade coat of arms.

So I told it over to myself, like the man I knew
Who lost three fingers on an oil rig when the well blew out.
"Lucky," he'd call himself, lift his hands in the taproom
   mirror,
Yell it out, "Lucky Seven," as if he knew what it meant.